Panoramic Journey Through
NAMIBIA

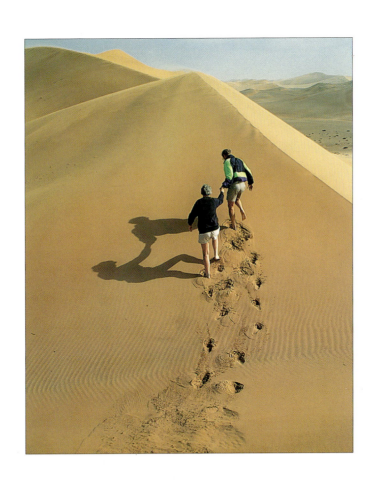

Panoramic Journey Through
NAMIBIA

First published in 2000 by Struik Publishers (Pty) Ltd
(a member of Struik New Holland Publishing (Pty) Ltd)

London • Cape Town • Sydney • Auckland

24 Nutford Place
London W1H 6DQ
United Kingdom

14 Aquatic Drive
Frenchs Forest
NSW 2086, Australia

80 McKenzie Street
Cape Town 8001
South Africa

218 Lake Road
Northcote, Auckland
New Zealand

10 9 8 7 6 5 4 3 2 1

Copyright © 2000 in published edition: Struik Publishers (Pty) Ltd
Copyright © 2000 in text: Alfred LeMaitre
Copyright © 2000 in photographs: Gerald Cubitt, with the exception of the following:
DB=Daryl Balfour; GI=Gallo Images; JdP=Jéan du Plessis; JK=Johan Kloppers; LPE=Leopard Photo Enterprises;
MH= Martin Harvey; PA=Photo Access; PL=Peter Lillie; PW=Patrick Wagner; SIL=Struik Image Library
Front cover (Walter Knirr), spine (Nigel J Dennis/GI), back cover (Richard du Toit); endpapers Getaway/
PW/PA); pages 1 (Richard du Toit); 2–3 (DB/GI); 5 (PL); 6 (JK/LPE); 9 (Rob Ponte/GI); 10 both (PW); 13 top
(Roger de la Harpe/GI), bottom (JK/LPE); 14 (JdP); 15 (JK/LPE); 17 both (JdP); 18 (Gerhard Dreyer/SIL);
21 right (Vanessa Burger/PA); 28 (PL); 30 (PL); 31 (Anthony Bannister/ GI); 32 left (JK/LPE), right (MH);
33 (GPL du Plessis/PA); 34 (JdP); 35 (PW); 36 top (JK/LPE), bottom and 37 (JdP); 38 (JL du Plessis);
39 (Charl Pauw); 40 (Thomas Dressler/GI); 41 bottom (Charl Pauw); 42 (PL); 43 (DB); 45 (Getaway/David
Bristow/PA); 51 (Mark Skinner); 56 (Alan Wilson/PA); 57 (Chanan Weiss); 58 (HPH Photography/PA); 59 left
(Fanie Kloppers/LPE), right (DB); 60 bottom (Vanessa Burger/PA); 61 (Chanan Weiss); 62 (PW); 63 bottom
(JdP); 64 top (JdP), bottom (Thomas Dressler/GI); 65 (DB/GI); 68 left (Roger de la Harpe/GI), right (JdP);
69 (MH); 70 and 71 (PL); 72 and 73 (MH); 75 and 76 (MH); 77 top (Rob Ponte/GI); 78 and 79 all (Getaway/
PW/PA); 80 (JK/LPE); 81 (Nigel J Dennis/GI); 82 left (JK/LPE), right and 82 (JdP); 84 (Peter Pickford/SIL);
85 top (JK/LPE), bottom (Getaway/PW/PA); 88 right (JdP); 90 and 91 (Anthony Bannister/GI).

DESIGNER Christelle Marais
EDITORS Inge du Plessis and Lesley Hay-Whitton
MANAGING EDITOR Annlerie van Rooyen
PICTURE RESEARCHER Carmen Watts
GERMAN TRANSLATOR Friedel Herrmann
FRENCH TRANSLATOR Jean-Paul Houssière

ISBN 1 86872 506 5

Reproduction by Hirt & Carter Cape (Pty) Ltd
Printed and bound by Craft Print Pte Ltd

All rights reserved. No part of this publication may be reproduced, stored in a retrieval system or transmitted,
in any form or by any means, electronic, mechanical, photocopying or otherwise, without the prior written
permission of the publishers and copyright holders.

ENDPAPERS *Sand dunes at Sossusvlei rise abruptly from the surrounding plains.*
PAGE 1 *Many climb Dune Seven in the Namib Desert outside Walvis Bay.*
PAGES 2–3 *Thirsty eland and kudu drink at a waterhole in Etosha National Park.*
RIGHT *After rain, a carpet of flowers graces the normally bone-dry pan at Sossusvlei.*

INTRODUCTION

Namibia offers some of southern Africa's most magnificent wilderness areas, among them the world-famous Etosha National Park, the Skeleton Coast Park and the huge Namib-Naukluft Park. In the far south, the Fish River Canyon is one of the world's largest canyons. The country has a diverse population, with a strong cultural influence remaining from the period of German colonial rule. With its immense open spaces and unspoiled natural beauty, sparsely populated Namibia beckons all those who appreciate untamed Africa.

EINFÜHRUNG

Namibia hat einige der beeindruckendsten Wildnisgebiete im südlichen Afrika aufzuweisen, wie den weltberühmten Etoscha-Nationalpark, den Skelettküsten-Nationalpark und den riesigen Namibib-Naukluft-Park. Im tiefen Süden liegt der Fischfluß-Cañon, einer der größten Cañons der Welt. Das Land ist ein Vielvölkerstaat, und aus der deutschen Kolonialzeit sind noch starke, kulturelle Strömungen zu verspüren. Mit seinen endlosen Flächen und der unverdorbenen Naturschönheit lockt das dünn besiedelte Namibia besonders jene, die sich für das ungezähmte Afrika begeistern.

INTRODUCTION

La Namibie possède quelques-unes unes des plus belles étendues sauvages de l'Afrique australe, parmi lesquelles on compte l'Etosha National Park, de renommée mondiale, le Skeleton Coast Park et l'immense Namib-Naukluft Park. Dans l'extrême Sud on trouvera le Fish River Canyon, un des plus grands du monde. La population du pays est diversifiée, et culturellement toujours influencée par l'époque coloniale allemande. Avec ses immenses espaces peu populeux et sa beauté naturelle toujours intacte, la Namibie attirera tous ceux qui sont épris de l'Afrique encore indomptée.

LEFT *From the rim, the Fish River Canyon presents one of Africa's most awe-inspiring sights.*
LINKS *Der Blick hinab in den Fischfluß-Canyon ist einer der überwältigensten in ganz Afrika.*
A GAUCHE *Vu du bord, le Fish River Canyon offre l'une des vues des plus impressionnantes d'Afrique.*

ABOVE *Isolated rocky hills rise from the dry, grassy plains around Grünau, in southeastern Namibia.*
OBEN *Hügelige Felseninseln ragen aus den trockenen Grasflächen empor bei Grünau, im südöstlichen Namibia.*
CI-DESSUS *Des saillies rocheuses émergent de la plaine près de Grünau, en Namibie du Sud-Est.*

ABOVE *The nests of sociable weaver birds are a common sight in telephone poles and trees in southern Namibia.*
OBEN *Die Nester der Siedelweber, an Telefonpfählen und Bäumen befestigt, sind ein häufiger Anblick im Süden Namibias.*
CI-DESSUS *Les nids de tisserins sont fréquents sur les poteaux téléphoniques et dans les arbres de la Namibie méridionale.*

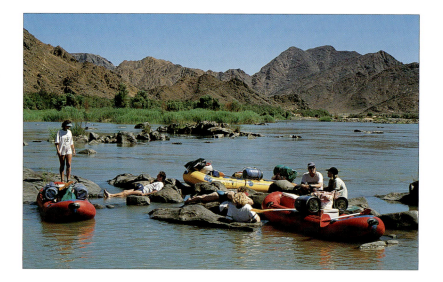

LEFT *A number of centres, like the one shown here, now offer rafting trips on the Gariep (Orange) River.*
LINKS *Einige Freizeitanlagen, wie das hier abgebildete, bieten jetzt Schlauchbootfahrten auf dem Gariep (Oranje) an.*
A GAUCHE *De nombreuses organisations offrent l'occasion de faire du rafting sur la Gariep (autrefois l'Orange).*

ABOVE *River rafting on the Gariep (Orange) is an increasingly popular activity for visitors to the region.*
OBEN *Schlauchbootfahrten auf dem Gariep (Oranje) erfreuen sich zunehmender Beliebtheit bei den Besuchern.*
CI-DESSUS *Les visiteurs dans la région sont de plus en plus nombreux à prendre part aux expéditions de rafting sur la Gariep.*

OPPOSITE *Thanks to intensive irrigation, vineyards now flourish along the banks of the Gariep (Orange).*
GEGENÜBER *Mit Hilfe von Bewässerungsanlagen gedeihen jetzt Weinfelder an den Ufern des Gariep (Oranje).*
CI-CONTRE *Grâce à l'irrigation, des vignobles s'épanouissent le long des rives de la Gariep.*

OPPOSITE *The mighty Fish River Canyon slices through the arid wilderness of southern Namibia.*
GEGENÜBER *Der gewaltige Fischfluß-Cañon schneidet durch die trockene Wildnis im südlichen Namibia.*
CI-CONTRE *L'imposant Fish River Canyon taillé dans l'étendue aride et sauvage du Sud de la Namibie.*

LEFT TOP *The Ai-Ais resort, at the southern end of the Fish River Canyon, is built around hot mineral springs.*
LINKS OBEN *Der Erholungsort Ai-Ais, am südlichen Ende des Fischfluß Cañons gelegen, ist um die mineralhaltigen Thermalquellen herum angelegt.*
CI-DESSUS, À GAUCHE *Le centre de Ais-Ais, à l'extrémité Sud du Fish River Canyon, est établi autour de sources d'eau minérales chaudes.*

LEFT *In winter, hikers undertake the 4- to 5-day journey through the canyon from Hobas to Ai-Ais.*
LINKS *In den Wintermonaten kann man 4- bis 5tägige Wanderungen von Hobas bis Ai-Ais durch den Cañon unternehmen.*
A GAUCHE *En hiver, par température modérée, les randonneurs suivent le canyon de Hobas jusqu'à Ais-Ais, une marche de 4 à 5 jours de long.*

ABOVE *A solitary wild horse grazes near Garub, on the route to Lüderitz.*
OBEN *Ein einsames Pferd weidet in der Nähe von Garub, auf dem Wege nach Lüderitz.*
CI-DESSUS *Un cheval solitaire broute près de Garub, sur la route de Lüderitz.*

RIGHT *The striking Quiver Tree (or Kokerboom) Forest is located outside the town of Keetmanshoop.*
RECHTS *Der beeindruckende Köcherbaumwald liegt außerhalb der Stadt Keetmanshoop.*
A DROITE *L'extraordinaire forêt de 'Quiver Tree' (ou kokerboom, arbre carquois) est située près de la ville de Keetmanshoop.*

OPPOSITE *The ghost town at Kolmanskop, one of several outside Lüderitz, is a reminder of the diamond rush of the early 1900s.*
GEGENÜBER *Die Geisterstadt Kolmanskop ist eine von mehreren, die im Umkreis von Lüderitz an den Diamantenrausch Anfang des 20. Jahrhunderts erinnert.*
CI-CONTRE *Kolmanskop une des villes mortes aux environs de Lüderitz, évoque l'époque de la ruée vers les diamants, au début du siècle passé.*

RIGHT TOP *The shifting sands of the Namib have invaded this house at Kolmanskop.*
RECHTS OBEN *Die Wanderdünen der Namib drangen auch in dieses Haus in Kolmanskop ein.*
CI-DESSUS À DROITE *Les sables mouvants du Namib ont envahi cette maison à Kolmanskop.*

RIGHT *An abandoned house at the Pomona ghost town preserves glimpses of a vanished way of life.*
RECHTS *Ein verlassenes Haus in der Geisterstadt Pomona gewährt einen Blick in eine vergangene Lebensweise.*
À DROITE *Cette maison en ruine dans la ville morte de Pomona, offre un aperçu d'un style de vie passé.*

ABOVE   *Offshore islands shelter colonies of chattering Cape gannets.*

OBEN   *Vorgelagerte Inseln bieten Kolonien der geschwätzigen Kaptölpel den nötigen Schutz.*

CI-DESSUS   *Les îles au large sont l'asile des fous de Bassan.*

RIGHT   *Sinclair Island, off the coast of the Diamond Area (closed to visitors), is favoured by large numbers of cormorants and jackass penguins.*

RECHTS   *Sinclair-Insel liegt vor der Diamantenküste (für Besucher gesperrt). Die Insel ist ein bevorzugtes Nistgebiet für Kormorane und Brillenpenguine.*

A DROITE   *Sinclair Island, au large de la 'Diamond Area (interdite au public) où de nombreux cormorans et pingouins se retrouvent.*

LEFT Also located within the Diamond Area is Bogenfels rock arch, a spectacular formation carved by the restless Atlantic waves.
LINKS Ebenfalls im Diamanten-Sperrgebiet ist der Bogenfels, eine eindrucksvolle Felsformation, die der ruhelose Atlantik hervorgebracht hat.
A GAUCHE Egalement située dans la 'Diamond Area', la voûte de Bogenfels est une étonnante sculpture créée par l'incessant mouvement des vagues et des marées de l'océan Atlantique.

OPPOSITE Tiny Plumpudding Island, off the coast of the Diamond Area, which is not open to visitors, was formerly exploited for its deposits of guano (nitrogen-rich bird droppings used for fertiliser).
GEGENÜBER 'Plumpudding' heißt die winzige Insel vor dem Küstenstreifen des Diamanten-Sperrgebiets. Hier erntete man früher Guano (stickstoffreicher Vogelmist, der als Düngemittel verwendet wird).
CI-CONTRE La minuscule Plumpudding Island, au large de la 'Diamond Area' (interdite au public), était autrefois exploitée pour ses dépôts de guano (excréments d'oiseaux riches en azote, et utilisés comme engrais).

ABOVE The Dias cross at Lüderitz is a replica of one set up here in 1487 by the Portuguese explorer Bartolomeu Dias.
OBEN Das Dias-Kreuz bei Lüderitz ist eine Nachbildung der ursprünglichen Kreuzsäule, die der portugiesische Entdeckungsreisende, Bartholomäus Diaz, 1487 hier errichtete.
CI-DESSUS La Croix de Dias à Lüderitz est une copie de l'original, érigé en ce même endroit en 1487 par l'explorateur portugais Bartolomé Dias.

ABOVE *Lüderitz boasts the country's finest natural harbour.*
OBEN *Lüderitz hat den besten, natürlichen Hafen des Landes.*
CI-DESSUS *Lüderitz s'enorgueillit du meilleur port naturel du pays.*

OPPOSITE *German colonial-era houses in Lüderitz.*
GEGENÜBER *Gebäude aus der deutschen Kolonialzeit in Lüderitz.*
CI-CONTRE *Habitations de l'ère coloniale allemande à Lüderitz.*

ABOVE *The resort at Hardap Dam is a welcome stop on the route between Keetmanshoop and Windhoek.*
OBEN *Der Erholungsort am Hardap-Stausee ist eine beliebte Zwischenstation auf dem Wege von Keetmanshoop nach Windhoek.*
CI-DESSUS *Hardap Dam, entre Keetmanshoop et Windhoek, est un centre de villégiature agréable où il est bon de faire étape.*

RIGHT *A distinctive line of palm trees in the Stampriet area, east of Mariental.*
RECHTS *Diese kennzeichnende Palmengruppe steht bei Stampriet, östlich von Mariental.*
A DROITE *Cette rangée de hauts palmiers agités par la brise légère, est une caractéristique de la région de Stampriet, à l'est de Mariental.*

ABOVE *Mule power is still a common sight in and around the town of Rehoboth, 'capital' of Namibia's Baster community.*

OBEN *Maulesel werden in und um Rehoboth, der 'Hauptstadt' der Bastergemeinde, noch häufig als Zugtiere verwendet.*

CI-DESSUS *La propulsion par mule est toujours d'usage courant à Rehoboth, la 'capitale' de la communauté des Baster en Namibie.*

LEFT *The Lutheran church in Rehoboth is a reminder of the town's early days as a Rhenish mission station.*
LINKS *Die lutherische Kirche in Rehoboth erinnert an die Frühzeit des Ortes als Rheinische Missionsstation.*
A GAUCHE *Le temple luthérien à Rheoboth évoque les jours de la domination coloniale allemande.*

ABOVE *The Baster people of the Rehoboth area are descended from Afrikaans-speaking migrants from the former Cape Colony.*
OBEN *Die Baster im Rehobothgebiet sind die Nachfahren Afrikaans sprechender Einwanderer, die aus der ehemaligen Kapkolonie hierhin gezogen waren.*
CI-DESSUS *Les Baster de Rheoboth descendent de travailleurs migrants afrikaans, venus de l'ancienne Colonie du Cap.*

ABOVE *Only the toughest of plants, such as the camelthorn tree, can survive in the arid wilderness conditions of the Namib Desert.*
OBEN *Nur die widerstandsfähigsten Pflanzen, wie der Kameldornbaum (Giraffenakazie), können in der trockenen Wildnis der Namibwüste überleben.*
CI-DESSUS *Seules les plantes les plus résistantes, comme le 'camelthorn', survivent dans l'aridité du désert du Namib.*

OPPOSITE *The great dune fields of the central Namib terminate abruptly along the Atlantic coast.*
GEGENÜBER *Die weitläufige Dünenlandschaft der Namib findet an der Atlantikküste ein jähes Ende.*
CI-CONTRE *Les fameuses dunes du Namib central se terminent brusquement sur le littoral atlantique.*

LEFT *The majestic gemsbok has evolved an efficient internal cooling system to withstand the harsh conditions of the Namib.*
LINKS *Die majestätische Oryxantilope hat ein wirksames, körpereigenes System zur Abkühlung entwickelt, um in dem gnadenlosen Umfeld der Namib zu überleben.*
A GAUCHE *Le majestueux gemsbok possède un excellent dispositif de refroidissement, qui lui permet d'endurer sans mal les rudes conditions du Namib.*

ABOVE *The sidewinding adder buries itself in the sand to conceal itself from prey.*
OBEN *Die Erdviper vergräbt sich im Sand, um sich vor Beutetieren zu verbergen.*
CI-DESSUS *Le crotale des sables se protège de ses attaquants en s'enfouissant sous la surface.*

LEFT *The sun-baked mud floor of the Dead Vlei at Sossusvlei is a reminder of the rare occasions when rains flood this dune-enclosed pan.*
LINKS *Die sonnenverbrannte Lehmkruste im Toten Teich bei Sossusvlei erinnert daran, daß es auch in dieser von Dünen umringten Pfanne hin und wieder zur Regenzeit Wasser gibt.*
A GAUCHE *Brûlé par le soleil, le fond boueux de Dead Vlei (étang mort) à Sossusvlei, rappelle que de rares pluies inondent cette dépression cernée de dunes.*

ABOVE *The desert-dwelling giant ground gecko uses its tongue to clean its face and eyes.*
OBEN *Der große Sandgecko, der sich Augen und Gesicht mit der Zunge reinigt, ist ein Wüstenbewohner.*
CI-DESSUS *Ce gecko, habitant du désert, se nettoie les yeux et la face en balayant avec sa langue.*

ABOVE *Skeletal tree trunks at Sossusvlei, in the Namib-Naukluft Park.*
OBEN *Skelettartige Baumstämme im Sossusvlei, in dem Namib-Naukluft-Park.*
CI-DESSUS *Troncs d'arbres squelettiques à Sossusvlei, dans le Namib-Naukluft Park.*

OPPOSITE *A convoy of 4x4 vehicles makes its way over the Namib dune fields.*
GEGENÜBER *Ein Geleitzug von Fahrzeugen mit Allradantrieb bahnt sich einen Weg durch die Dünenlandschaft der Namib.*
CI-CONTRE *Un convoi de véhicules 4x4 franchi laborieusement les dunes du Namib.*

LEFT *Hot-air ballooning is a novel, and increasingly popular, way of appreciating the immense sweep of the Namib.*
LINKS *Ausflüge im Heißluftballon bieten eine neuartige und immer beliebtere Art, die endlosen Weiten der Namib zu betrachten.*
A GAUCHE *La montgolfière est un des moyens les plus originaux, et de plus en plus populaire, permettant d'apprécier l'immensité du Namib.*

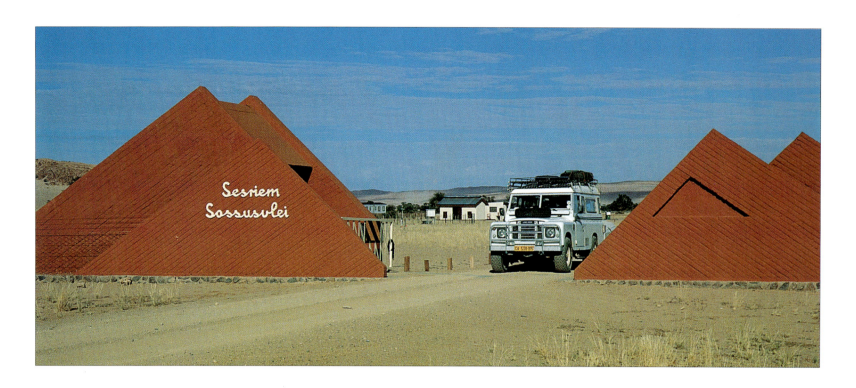

ABOVE *From the Sesriem entrance to the Namib-Naukluft Park, a good gravel road leads to the dunes at Sossusvlei.*
OBEN *Von dem Eingang zum Namib-Naukluft-Park bei Sesriem führt eine gute Schotterpiste zu den Dünen am Sossusvlei.*
CI-DESSUS *Une bonne piste gravillonnée va de l'entrée de Sesriem au Namib-Naukluft Park, aux dunes de Sossusvlei.*

RIGHT *Accommodation at the popular Karos Lodge at Sesriem – entrance to one of the four sections of the Namib-Naukluft Park – is inspired by North African village architecture.*

RECHTS *In der beliebten Karos Lodge in Sesriem – Pforte zu einer der vier Regionen des Namib-Naukluft-Parks – sind die Unterkünfte in der Bauweise nordafrikanischer Dörfer gehalten.*

A DROITE *Le populaire Karos Lodge à Sesriem est aussi l'entrée d'une des quatre sections du Namib-Naukluft Park; le style de l'architecture est d'inspiration Nord africaine.*

OPPOSITE BOTTOM *A group of outdoor enthusiasts having a break on the Namib-Naukluft's specialised 4x4 trail.*

GEGENÜBER UNTEN *Für Liebhaber von Fahr-zeugen mit Allradantrieb bietet der Namib-Naukluft-Park besondere Strecken.*

CI-CONTRE, CI-DESSOUS *Les fervents de 4x4 trouveront au Namib-Naukluft des pistes créées spécialement à leur intention.*

BELOW *A stroll along the shore is the best way to see the large colony of lesser flamingoes at Sandwich Harbour, south of Walvis Bay.*
UNTEN *Die riesige Kolonie der Zwergflamingos bei Sandwich Harbour, läßt sich bei einem Strandspaziergang gut beobachten.*
CI-DESSOUS *Le meilleur moyen d'observer l'importante colonie de flamants à Sandwich Harbour est une promenade sur la plage.*

OPPOSITE *The lagoon system at Sandwich Harbour is an important habitat, both for marine creatures and birds.*
GEGENÜBER *Die Lagunenwelt bei Sandwich Harbour, südlich von Walvis Bay, ist ein wichtiges Habitat für viele Meerestiere und Vögel.*
CI-CONTRE *Le réseau de lagons de Sandwich Harbour est un important habitat pour les oiseaux et les créatures marines.*

ABOVE *Walvis Bay, an important harbour and bird-watcher's paradise, was a South African port until the early 1990s.*
OBEN *Walvis Bay, ein wichtiger Hafen und ein Paradies für Boebachter von Vögeln, war bis Mitte der neunziger Jahre noch eine südafrikanische Enklave.*
CI-DESSUS *Walvis Bay était un port sud-africain jusqu'au début des années 1990; c'est aussi un paradis pour les ornithologues.*

LEFT *Walvis Bay's fishing trawlers ply the cold, nutrient-rich offshore waters in search of pilchards and whitefish.*

LINKS *Die Hochseeflotte von Walvis Bay kreist in den kalten, nahrungsreichen Küstengewässern umher, auf der Suche nach Schwärmen von Sardinen und Weißfisch.*

A GAUCHE *Les chalutiers de Walvis Bay sillonnent les eaux froides et poissonneuses au large, à la recherche du pilchard et du poisson blanc.*

BELOW *Pelican Point lighthouse has long been a reassuring landmark for sailors entering the anchorage at Walvis Bay.*

UNTEN *Der Leuchtturm von Pelican Point wird schon seit sehr langer Zeit von Seefahrern, die sich der Reede von Walvis Bay nähern, als willkom-menes Wahrzeichen begrüßt.*

CI-DESSOUS *Le phare de Pelican Point a toujours été un repère bienvenu pour les marins pénétrant le mouillage de Walvis Bay.*

THIS SPREAD *The strange Welwitschia plant, found only in the Namib, can attain an immense age. Amazingly, the plant has only two, long leaves. The male plant* (RIGHT) *is markedly different from the female* (ABOVE).

DIESE SEITEN *Die seltsame Welwitschia, die nur in der Namib anzutreffen ist, kann uralt werden. Verblüffenderweise hat die Pflanze nur zwei lange Blätter. Männliche Pflanzen* (RECHTS) *unterscheiden sich deutlich von weiblichen* (OBEN).

CES DEUX PAGES *L'étrange welwitschia ne se trouve que dans le Namib et peut atteindre un âge étonnant. Fait surprenant: elle n'a que deux longues feuilles. La plante male* (À DROITE) *est nettement différente de la femelle* (CI-DESSUS).

OPPOSITE *The popular seaside resort of Swakopmund is situated 31 kilometres north of the industrial town of Walvis Bay.*
GEGENÜBER *Swakopmund, der beliebte Ferienort an der Küste, liegt 31km nördlich von der Industriestadt, Walvis Bay.*
CI-CONTRE *Une vue aérienne de la populaire station balnéaire de Swakopmund, située à 31km au nord de Walvis Bay..*

ABOVE *Hohenzollern House is one of the grandest of Swakopmund's colonial-era buildings.*
OBEN *Haus Hohenzollern ist wohl das prächtigste der alten Gebäude aus der Kolonialzeit.*
CI-DESSUS *Sans doute l'immeuble le plus grandiose de l'ère coloniale à Swakopmund: Hohenzollern House.*

LEFT *Although the Atlantic waters are chilly, Swakopmund's fine sandy beach provides year-round recreation.*

LINKS *Obgleich das Meerwasser des Atlantik kalt ist, bietet der herrliche Sandstrand von Swakopmund das ganze Jahr hindurch Erholung.*

A GAUCHE *Malgré les eaux froides de l'Atlantique, le climat est tel que l'on peut profiter des belles plages sablonneuses de Swakopmund toute l'année durant.*

OPPOSITE *Camels, first brought to Namibia in colonial times, offer a novel mode of exploring the Namib near Swakopmund.*

GEGENÜBER *Kamele wurden erstmals zur Kolonialzeit nach Namibia gebracht; jetzt bieten sie eine ungewöhnliche Art, die Wüste um Swakopmund zu erkunden.*

CI-CONTRE *Le chameau, initialement introduit durant l'ère coloniale, offre aujourd'hui un moyen original pour explorer le Namib, dans les environs de Swakopmund.*

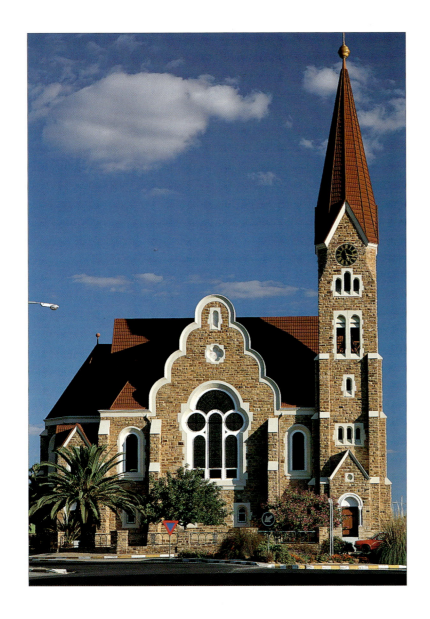

LEFT *Windhoek's Christuskirche, consecrated in 1910, is one of the city's oldest structures.*
LINKS *Die Christuskirche in Windhoek wurde 1910 geweiht und ist somit eines der ältesten Gebäude der Stadt.*
A GAUCHE *Christuskirche, consacrée en 1910, est un des édifices les plus anciens de Windhoek.*

ABOVE *The white-walled Alte Feste (Old Fort), with the Rider Memorial in the foreground, is part of Namibia's State Museum.*
OBEN *Die Alte Feste, umgeben von weißen Mauern und mit dem Reiterdenkmal im Vordergrund, bildet Teil des Staatsmuseums von Namibia.*
CI-DESSUS *Le vieux fort aux murailles blanches 'Alte Feste', avec, à l'avant plan le 'Rider Memorial', fait partie du musée national de Namibie.*

OPPOSITE *Windhoek, capital of Namibia, is a pleasant, modern city surrounded by a chain of low hills.*
GEGENÜBER *Windhoek, die Hauptstadt Namibias, ist eine freundliche, moderne Stadt, umgeben von einer Hügelkette.*
CI-CONTRE *La capitale de Namibie, Windhoek, est une ville moderne et agréable, entourée de collines.*

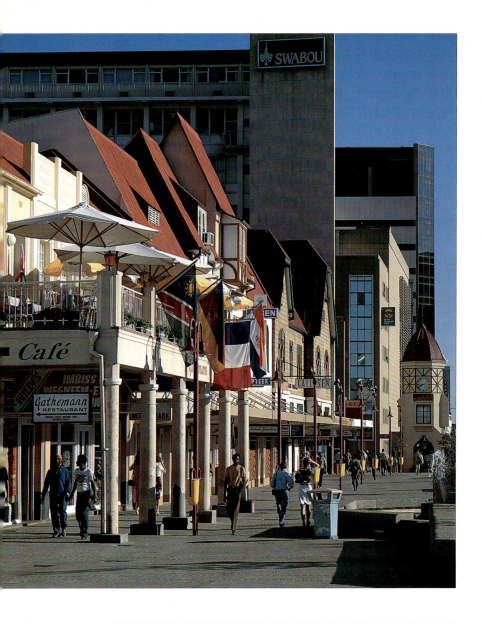

ABOVE *Wambo basketwork laid out for sale on a sidewalk in Windhoek.*
OBEN *Korbwaren aus Ovamboland werden auf dem Bürgersteig in Windhoek zum Verkauf angeboten.*
CI-DESSUS *Un étalage de vannerie Wambo sur un trottoir de Windhoek.*

ABOVE *The buildings in Windhoek's shopping centre show the city's German heritage.*
OBEN *Die Einkaufsstraßen von Windhoek reflektieren deutlich das deutsche Erbe dieser Stadt.*
CI-DESSUS *Les rues commerçantes de Windhoek ne laissent aucun doute quant au patrimoine allemand de la ville.*

OPPOSITE *The costumes worn by many Herero women recall the garb of 19th-century German missionaries.*
GEGENÜBER *Die Tracht der Hererofrauen ist auf die Kleidung der deutschen Missionarsfrauen im 19. Jahrhundert zurück zu führen.*
CI-CONTRE *Les costumes portés par de nombreuses femmes Herero rappellent l'habit des missionnaires allemands du 19ième.*

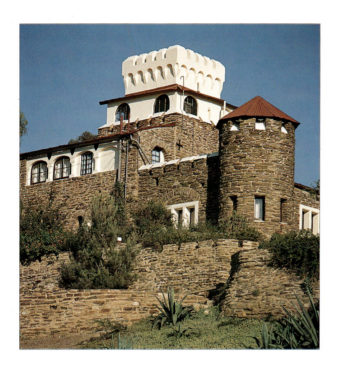

ABOVE *Schwerinsburg Castle, a private residence, is a fanciful construction built on the foundations of an old German fort.*

OBEN *Schwerinsburg, ein privates Wohnhaus, ist eine eigenwillige Konstruktion, die auf den Fundamenten einer alten Festung errichtet wurde.*

CI-DESSUS *Cette propriété privée, le chëteau de Schweringsburg, est une élaboration fantasque érigée sur les fondations d'un ancien fort allemand.*

RIGHT *The rest camp in the Daan Viljoen Game Reserve occupies a pleasant corner of the Khomas hills west of Windhoek.*

RECHTS *Das Rastlager im Daan Viljoen Wildpark liegt in einer reizvollen Ecke der hügeligen Khomaslandschaft, westlich von Windhoek.*

A DROITE *Le camp de la réserve Daan Viljoen est idéalement situé dans les collines de Khomas, à l'ouest de Windhoek.*

OPPOSITE *Trails Camp nestles among the weathered sandstone pinnacles of the Waterberg Plateau Park.*
GEGENÜBER *Zwischen den verwitterten Sandsteingipfeln im Waterberg-Plateau-Naturpark nestelt das Rastlager 'Trails Camp'.*
CI-CONTRE *Trails Camp est niché parmi les anciens pics de grès au Waterberg Plateau Park.*

ABOVE *Visitors to the luxurious Mount Etjo Safari Lodge can view big game from the comfort of a ranger-driven vehicle.*
OBEN *Die Besucher der luxuriösen Mount Etjo Safari Lodge können von dem Geländewagen aus bequem Großwild beobachten.*
CI-DESSUS *A Mount Etjo Safari Lodge, les visiteurs peuvent observer les animaux sauvages en tout confort, dans un véhicule spécial.*

LEFT *The fang-like Gross Spitzkoppe rears above the neighbouring rocky hills.*
LINKS *Wie riesige Zähne aus Gestein ragt die Gross-Spitzkoppe über die felsigen Hügel der Umgebung hinaus.*
A GAUCHE *Comme un croc inquiétant, le Gross Spitzkoppe surgit au-dessus des sommets rocheux voisins.*

ABOVE *The rugged landscape of the Spitzkoppe is a paradise for rock-climbers.*
OBEN *Die zerklüftete Landschaft in der Umgebung der Spitzkoppe ist ein Paradies für Bergsteiger.*
CI-DESSUS *Le terrain accidenté de Spitzkoppe est un paradis pour les varappeurs.*

ABOVE This impressive natural rock arch is located in the Spitzkoppe region, northeast of Swakopmund.
OBEN Diesen eindrucksvollen Bogenfels kann man bei der Spitzkoppe bewundern.
CI-DESSUS Cette magnifique voûte rocheuse est située dans la région de Spitzkoppe.

OPPOSITE RIGHT Normally nocturnal, leopards are the lords of the upland areas of wild Namibia.
GEGENÜBER, RECHTS Die generell nachtaktiven Leoparden beherrschen die Hochlandregionen der Wildnisgebiete Namibias.
CI-CONTRE, À DROITE Normalement un animal nocturne, le léopard règne suprême dans les hautes terres de la Namibie sauvage.

BELOW *These dinosaur footprints, found on a farm outside the town of Kalkfeld, were made more than 150 million years ago.*
UNTEN *Diese Fußabdrücke eines Dinosauriers, die man auf einer Farm bei Kalkfeld fand, sind mehr als 150 Millionen Jahre alt.*
CI-DESSOUS *Ces empreintes de dinosaure, découvertes près de la ville de Kalkfeld, ont été laissées il y a plus de 150 millions d'années.*

RIGHT *An ancient rock engraving at Twyfelfontein, in Damaraland, portrays an elephant, among other creatures.*
RECHTS *Eine uralte Felsgravierung bei Twyfelfontein im Damaraland zeigt einen Elefanten und andere Tierarten.*
A DROITE *Une ancienne gravure rupestre à Twyfelfontein, au Damaraland, représente un éléphant, entre autres créatures.*

RIGHT BOTTOM *As the rock cooled, many millions of years ago, the Organ Pipes at Twyfelfontein assumed this distinctive columnar formation.*
RECHTS UNTEN *Als die Felsen über Jahrmillionen hinweg abkühlten, bildeten sich diese eigenartigen Säulenformationen bei Twyfelfontein, die als Orgelpfeifen bekannt sind.*
CI-DESSOUS, À DROITE *Twyfelfontein, les 'Organ Pipes' (tuyaux d'orgue). Cette formation de colonnes rocheuses fut créée il y a des millions d'années, par le refroidissement du roc.*

OPPOSITE *The rugged Twyfelfontein region, with its more than 2,400 rock engravings, is one of the world's great open-air art galleries.*
GEGENÜBER *Das zerklüftete Gebiet bei Twyfelfontein ist mit über 2,400 Felsgravierungen eine riesige Freilicht-Gallerie.*
CI-CONTRE *La région de Twyfelfontein, qui possède plus de 2,400 gravures rupestres, est l'une des plus vastes galeries d'art en plein air.*

OPPOSITE *Damaraland's open spaces are an invitation to exploration and adventure. Brandberg (Burnt Mountain) east of Twyfelfontein is stark and forbidding.*
GEGENÜBER *Die ausgedehnten Flächen des Damaralandes locken zum Erkunden und Erleben. Der Brandberg, östlich von Twyfelfontein, ist ein imposanter und fast bedrohlicher Anblick.*
CI-CONTRE *Les grands espaces libres du Damaraland sont une invitation à l'exploration et l'aventure. Brandberg (la montagne brûlée) à l'est de Twyfelfontein, a un aspect désolé et inhospitalier.*

RIGHT TOP *On a rocky overhang deep in the rugged Brandberg massif is a collection of San rock paintings, including the well-known and misnamed White Lady.*
RECHTS OBEN *Tief in dem zerklüfteten Brandberg haben San Künstler viele Felsmalereien hinterlassen, einschließlich der wohl berühmtesten, die fälschlicherweise als die 'Weiße Dame' bekannt ist.*
CI-DESSUS, À DROITE *Sur un surplomb rocheux au cour du massif de Brandberg, on trouvera une collection d'art rupestre San, comprenant la bien connue, mais appelée à tort, 'White Lady'.*

RIGHT *A humble dwelling displays images of northern Namibia's wealth of game species.*
RECHTS *Selbst diese dürftige Behausung deutet auf den Wildreichtum im Norden Namibias.*
À DROITE *Cette humble chaumière est décorée d'images représentant la diversité de la faune de la Namibie septentrionale.*

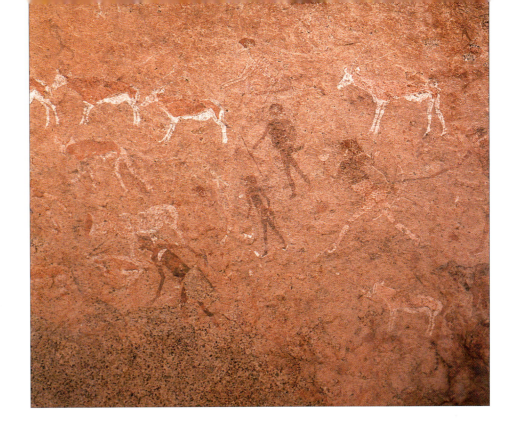

LEFT *The symbol on this gate in the Skeleton Coast Park is a reminder of the harsh conditions in this arid wilderness.*
LINKS *Die abschreckende Abbildung auf dem Tor weist Besucher des Skelettküsten-Nationalparks auf die gnadenlosen Lebensbedingungen in dieser öden Wildnis.*
A GAUCHE *Le symbole macabre à l'entrée du Skeleton Coast Park ne laisse aucun doute quant aux conditions difficiles existant dans cette région aride.*

LEFT BOTTOM *Shifting sands mean treacherous driving conditions along the Skeleton Coast.*
LINKS UNTEN *Sandverwehungen machen das Autofahren an der Skelettküste schwierig und gefährlich.*
CI-DESSOUS, À GAUCHE *Des sables mouvants rendent la conduite très dangereuse au long de la Skeleton Coast.*

OPPOSITE *Although rain seldom falls in the Skeleton Coast, this oasis shows there is water under the desert.*
GEGENÜBER *Obgleich es an der Skelettküste praktisch nie regnet, beweist diese kleine Oase, daß unter der Wüstenoberfläche Wasser vorhanden ist.*
CI-CONTRE *Bien qu'il pleuve rarement sur la Skeleton Coast, cette petite oasis démontre qu'il y a de l'eau sous la surface du désert.*

FOLLOWING PAGES *The Skeleton Coast takes its name from the many ships claimed by its reefs and sandbars.*
NACHFOLGENDE SEITEN *Die Skelettküste verdankt ihren Namen den vielen Schiffswracks, die ihren Felsenriffen und Sandbänken zum Opfer gefallen sind.*
PAGES SUIVANTES *Le nom 'Skeleton Coast' vient des nombreuses épaves de bateaux qui ont fait naufrage sur ses récifs et bancs de sable.*

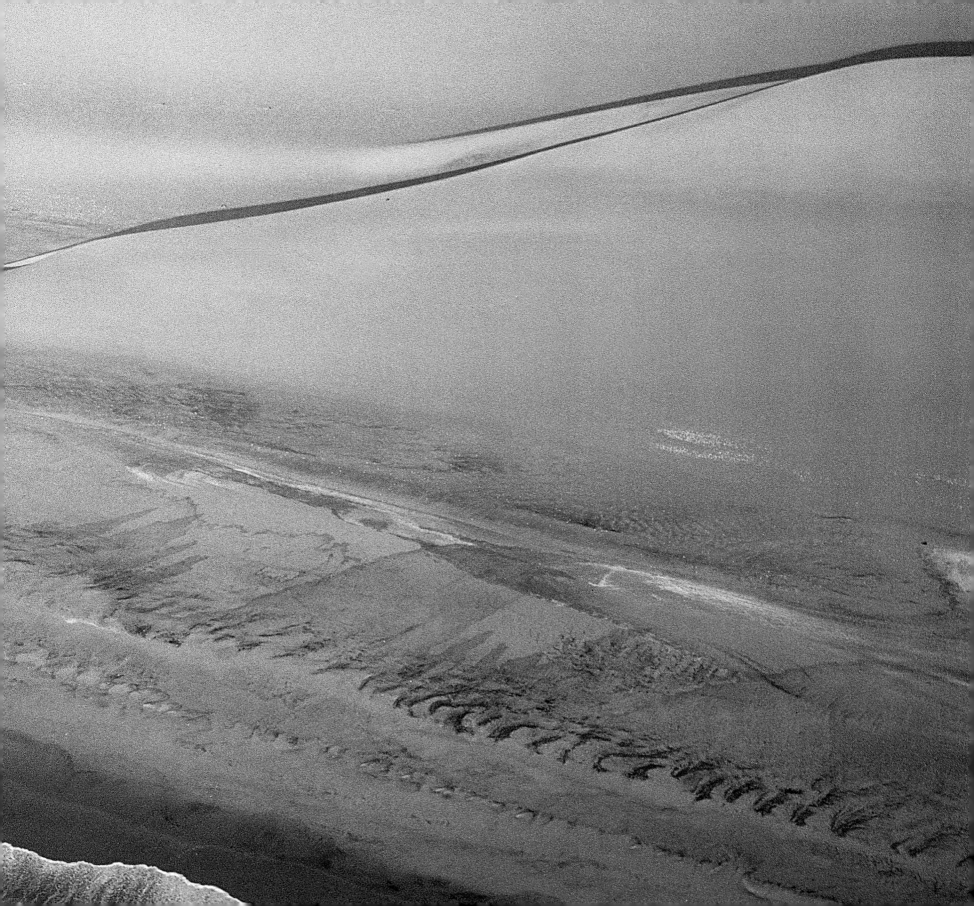

ABOVE *The elusive black-backed jackal scavenges the tideline of the Skeleton Coast in search of food.*
OBEN *Der Schabrackenschakal sucht auf dem Gezeitenstrand an der Skelettküste nach Eßbarem.*
CI-DESSUS *Le chacal à dos noir explore la ligne de marée sur la Skeleton Coast, à la recherche de nourriture.*

ABOVE *Cape Cross is named for the cross that was erected here in 1485 by the Portuguese explorer Diego Cão.*
OBEN *Der Name Kreuzkap bezieht sich auf die Kreuzsäule, die 1485 von dem portugiesischen Entdeckungsreisenden Diego Cão hier errichtet wurde.*
CI-DESSUS *Cape Cross, ainsi nommé d'après la croix érigée en cet endroit par l'explorateur portugais Diego Cão en 1485.*

OPPOSITE *Cape fur seals are found in abundance along the Namibian coast.*
GEGENÜBER *Kap Pelzrobben sind an der Küste Namibias in großer Zahl anzutreffen.*
CI-CONTRE *Les phoques sont très abondants tout au long de la côte namibienne.*

OPPOSITE *Elephant approach a waterhole in Etosha National Park.*
GEGENÜBER *Elefanten nähern sich im Trab einer Wasserstelle im Etoscha-Nationalpark.*
CI-CONTRE *Des éléphants se précipitent à l'approche d'un point d'eau à Etosha Game Park, soulevant la poussière.*

BELOW *Burchell's zebra, one of the many game species seen in Etosha.*
UNTEN *Burchell-Zebra zählen zu den vielen Wildarten, die den Etoscha-Nationalpark bevölkern.*
CI-DESSOUS *Des zèbres de Burchell, une des nombreuses espèces qui se rassemblent à l'Etosha National Park.*

LEFT *The need for water enforces peaceful coexistence.*
LINKS *Das lebensnotwendige Wasser erzwingt ein friedliches Nebeneinander der Geschöpfe.*
A GAUCHE *Le besoin de se désaltérer impose la coexistence pacifique pour toute créature.*

ABOVE *Taking a drink is a serious business for a giraffe.*
OBEN *Trinken ist für Giraffen ein schwieriges Unterfangen.*
CI-DESSUS *Pour une girafe, 'prendre un verre' est une affaire sérieuse.*

ABOVE *One of Etosha's male lions waits in the shade for a hunting opportunity.*
OBEN *Ein männlicher Löwe wartet im Schatten auf die Gelegenheit zu einem Beutezug.*
CI-DESSUS *Etosha. Un lion patiente à l'ombre, attendant l'arrivée d'une proie.*

RIGHT *In summer, huge numbers of game are attracted to Etosha's life-giving waterholes.*
RECHTS *Riesige Wildherden ziehen in den Sommermonaten zu den lebensspendenden Wasserstellen im Etoscha-Nationalpark.*
A DROITE *En été, de grandes quantités d'animaux sont attirés par les points d'eau vitaux d'Etosha.*

ABOVE *Etosha's Okaukuejo waterhole is a fine spot for game-viewing. At night, the waterhole is lit by floodlights.*

OBEN *Das Wasserloch bei Okaukuejo in Etoscha ist ein günstiger Fleck zur Wildbeobachtung. Bei Nacht wird diese Wasserstelle angestrahlt.*

CI-DESSUS *Etosha. Le point d'eau d'Okaukuejo est excellent pour observer les animaux. A la nuit tombée, l'endroit est éclairé à l'électricité.*

LEFT *Etosha's Namutoni camp is housed in an old German colonial fort.*
LINKS *Namutoni, die alte Feste aus deutscher Kolonialzeit, bildet Teil der Unterkünfte in diesem Rastlager in Etoscha.*
A GAUCHE *Cet ancien fort colonial allemand fait partie de Namutoni, un des trois camps à Etosha.*

BELOW *The view from the tower at Okaukuejo reveals the camp's modern facilities and the game-rich plains beyond.*
UNTEN *Vom Turm in Okaukuejo blickt man auf die modernen Anlagen des Rastlagers und auf die wildreichen Ebenen, die sich dahinter erstrecken.*
CI-DESSOUS *Cette vue d'Okaukuejo montre les aménagements modernes du camp, et, dans le fond, les plaines où abondent les animaux.*

OPPOSITE *At Epupa Falls, on Namibia's border with Angola, the Kunene River rushes through a narrow cleft in the surrounding rocks.*
GEGENÜBER *Bei den Epupa-Fällen, an der Grenze zu Angola, stürzt der Kunene in eine Gesteinsspalte der umliegenden Felsen.*
CI-CONTRE *Epupa Falls, sur la frontière entre l'Angola et la Namibie, où la Kunene se précipite dans une étroite fissure dans le roc.*

RIGHT TOP *Rafters on the Kunene River take a moment to chat with a group of Himba, the people of Kaokoland.*
RECHTS OBEN *Schlauchbootfahrer auf dem Kunene verweilen einen Augenblick, um mit einer Gruppe Himba, der einheimischen Bevölkerung im Kaokoland, zu plaudern.*
CI-DESSUS, À DROITE *Des amateurs de rafting s'entretiennent avec un groupe de Himba, peuple indigène du Kaokoland.*

RIGHT *The Kunene offers some thrilling opportunities for white-water canoeing.*
RECHTS *Der Kunene bietet tolle Möglichkeiten für Kanufahrten über Stromschnellen.*
A DROITE *Les eaux torrentueuses de la Kunene offrent des moments palpitants pour les canoéistes en eau vive.*

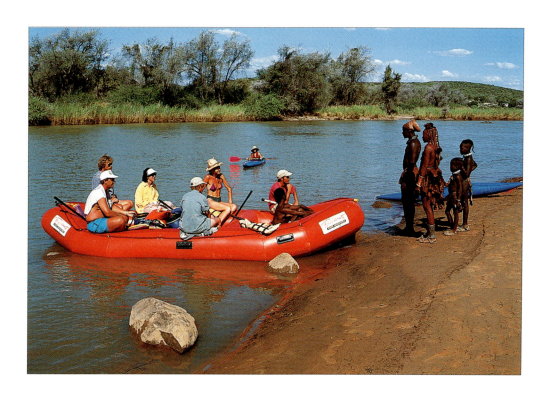

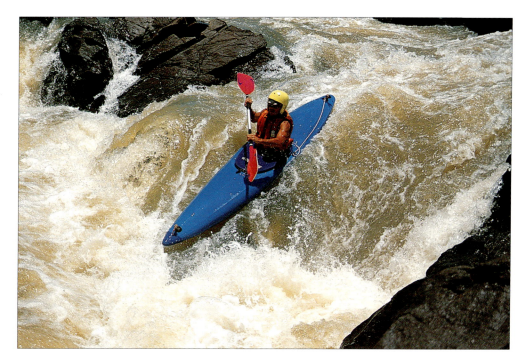

ABOVE *Himba dwellings are made of a cone of saplings plastered with cattle dung.*
OBEN *Die Rundhütten der Himba haben eine Rahmenstruktur aus Zweigen, die mit Kuhmist verputzt wird.*
CI-DESSUS *Les Himba construisent leurs huttes avec des branches enduites de bouse de vache.*

RIGHT *A herd of desert-dwelling elephants approaches a deserted Himba village in the barren Kaokoveld region of northwestern Namibia.*
RECHTS *Eine Herde Wüstenelefanten nähert sich einem verlassenen Himbadorf in der kargen Landschaft des Kaokoland im Nordwesten Namibias.*
A DROITE *Au Kaokoland, un troupeau d'éléphants du désert arrive à un village himba abandonné.*

LEFT *This Himba mother and her child wear traditional clothes of softened calfskin coated with ochre.*

LINKS *Diese Himbamutter und ihr Kind tragen die traditionelle Kleidung, die aus weich gegerbtem und mit Ockerfarbe bedecktem Kalbsleder angefertigt wird.*

A GAUCHE *Cette jeune mère Himba et son enfant portent leurs accoutrements traditionnels en vachette recouverte d'ocre.*

ABOVE *Body ornamentation, particularly making use of shells, metal and leather, is integral to the Himba way of life.*

OBEN *Körperschmuck, besonders aus Muscheln, Metall und Leder hergestellt, gehört zum Brauchtum der Himba.*

CI-DESSUS *Les ornements corporels, spécialement les coquillages, métaux et cuir, sont intrinsèques au style de vie Himba.*

BELOW *A Himba woman busies herself with household chores. The Himba, related to the Herero people of northeastern Namibia, still follow a semi-nomadic way of life based on herding cattle.*
UNTEN *Eine Himbafrau bei der Hausarbeit. Die Himba sind mit dem Hererovolk verwandt, das im Nordosten Namibias lebt, und sie führen weiterhin ein halb-nomadisches Dasein, das auf Rinderzucht basiert.*
CI-DESSOUS *Une Himba faisant le ménage. Les Himba sont apparentés aux Herero du Nord-Est de la Namibie. Leur mode de vie est celui des nomades, principalement la garde des troupeaux.*

OPPOSITE *The Himba make their homes in the beautiful but harsh Kaokoveld.*
GEGENÜBER *Die Himba haben sich in dem herrlichen, aber gnadenlosen Kaokoland ihre Heimat geschaffen.*
CI-CONTRE *Les Himba se sont établis dans le Kaokoveld, une belle, mais rigoureuse région dans le Nord-Ouest de la Namibie.*

LEFT TOP *A Himba man summons his herd using a blower made from a gemsbok horn.*
LINKS OBEN *Ein Himbamann sammelt seine Herde mit einem Blasinstrument aus Oryxhorn.*
CI-DESSUS, À GAUCHE *Cet Himba appelle son troupeau en soufflant dans une corne de gemsbok.*

LEFT *For the Himba, the Kunene River is an important avenue of transportation.*
LINKS *Der Kunene bildet für die Himba eine wichtige Verkehrsader.*
À GAUCHE *La Kunene est une importante voie d'eau pour les Himba.*

85

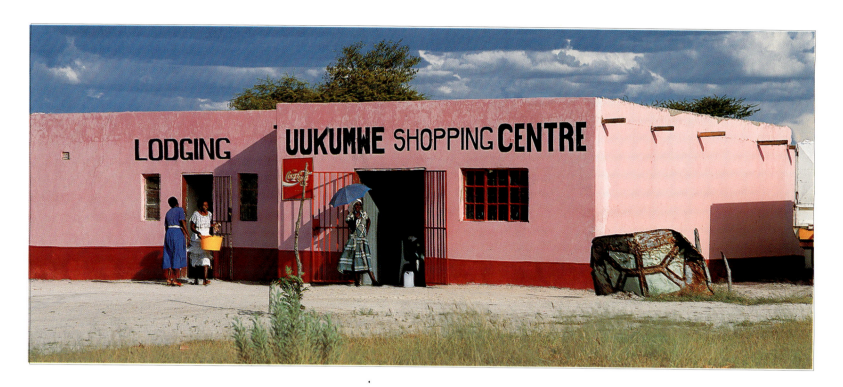

ABOVE *Shopping centres such as this one serve the Wambo people of Ovamboland, the most populous region of Namibia.*

OBEN *Kleine Einkaufszentren, wie dieses, versorgen die Bevölkerung im Ovamboland, das die dichtbesiedelste Region Namibias ist.*

CI-DESSUS *Ce petit centre commercial est typique de ceux qui desservent les Wambo en Ovamboland, la région la plus populeuse de Namibie.*

RIGHT *Local industries, like this machine shop outside Oshakati, flourish in Ovamboland.*

RECHTS *Heimwerkstätten, wie diese für Gerätschaften und Möbel, machen gute Geschäfte.*

A DROITE *Les petites industries locales, comme cet atelier d'usinage à Oshakati, prospèrent en Ovamboland.*

ABOVE *Cattle herding is an important activity in Ovamboland, which enjoys an abundance of water relative to the rest of the country.*
OBEN *Rinderhüten ist eine wichtige Tätigkeit in Ovamboland, wo es – im Verhältnis zu dem Rest des Landes – reichlich Wasser gibt.*
CI-DESSUS *Comparé au reste du pays, l'eau abonde en Ovamboland, et l'élevage du bétail est une des activités principales.*

LEFT *The Kavango people of northeastern Namibia use woven basketwork cones to catch fish in the Kavango River.*
LINKS *Das Volk der Kavango im Nordosten Namibias benutzt trichterförmige Körbe zum Fischfang im Kavangofluß.*
A GAUCHE *Les Kavango, dans le Nord-Est de la Namibie, utilisent des nasses d'osier pour pêcher dans la Kavango.*

ABOVE *The town of Nyangana, at the western margin of the Caprivi Strip, is home to a Roman Catholic mission.*
OBEN *In Nyangana, im westlichen Caprivi-Streifen, ist eine katholische Missionsstation angesiedelt.*
CI-DESSUS *Cette jolie mission catholique est à Nyangana, une petite ville située à l'extrémité ouest de Caprivi Strip.*

OPPOSITE *Fishermen use mokoros (dugout canoes) to ply the Kavango, which is called the Okavango after it enters neighbouring Botswana.*
GEGENÜBER *Die Flußfischer benutzen Mokoros (Einbaumkanus) auf dem Kavango, der im benachbarten Botswana dann Okavango genannt wird.*
CI-CONTRE *Les pêcheurs sillonnent la Kavango en mukoros (pirogues); en entrant le Botswana, la rivière change de nom et devient la Okavango.*

RIGHT *Gathering edible wild plants is part of the traditional way of life of Namibia's San community.*

RECHTS *Das Sammeln eßbarer Wildpflanzen gehört zur traditionellen Lebensweise der zahlreichen San-Bevölkerung Namibias, die früher als Buschleute bekannt waren.*

A DROITE *La cueillette de plantes sauvages comestibles est une des traditions de l'importante tribu des San de Namibie.*

OPPOSITE *San men prepare poison arrows for use in hunting game. Although famed for their ability to live off the land, decreasing numbers of San now still follow a lifestyle of hunting and gathering.*

GEGENÜBER *Die San verwenden Giftpfeile zur Jagd. Obwohl sie gerade dafür bekannt sind, daß sie in der Wildnis überleben können, nimmt die Zahl der San, die noch ein Jäger- und-Sammler-Leben führt, ständig ab.*

CI-CONTRE *Chasseurs San préparant des flèches empoisonnées. Bien qu'ils soient renommés pour leur aptitude à vivre de la terre, les San sont de plus en plus nombreux à abandonner leurs traditions ancestrales.*

90

91

OPPOSITE *A group of herders bring their cattle back to the village of Kalembeza, in Namibia's distant East Caprivi province.*
GEGENÜBER *Eine Gruppe von Viehhirten geleitet ihre Rinder zurück zu dem Dorf Kalembeza, das in der abgelegenen Provinz von Ost-Kaprivi liegt.*
CI-CONTRE *Des gardiens de troupeaux retournent avec leur bétail à Kalembeza, un village dans la distante province Namibienne de Caprivi.*

ABOVE *At Katima Mulilo, the Zambezi Lodge's floating bar offers a tranquil place to contemplate the mighty Zambezi River.*
OBEN *Bei Katima Mulilo bietet die schwimmende Bar der Zambezi Lodge ein geruhsames Plätzchen, um den mächtigen Sambesi auf sich einwirken zu lassen.*
CI-DESSUS *Le bar flottant de la Zambezi Lodge à Katima Mulilo, est un endroit serein pour contempler l'imposant Zambèze.*

ABOVE *The enchanting carmine bee-eater dwells in the woodlands and savanna of northeastern Namibia and the Caprivi Strip.*
OBEN *Der bezaubernde Scharlachspint ist in den Gras- und Baumsavannen im nordöstlichen Namibia und im Caprivi-Streifen beheimatet.*
CI-DESSUS *Ce charmant mangeur d'abeilles réside dans les forêts et la savane du Nord-Est de la Namibie, et dans le Caprivi Strip.*

RIGHT *Visitors can observe East Caprivi's abundant birdlife from the comfort of Lianshulu Lodge's double-decker observation boat.*
RECHTS *Besucher im Ost-Caprivi können das reichhaltige Vogelleben von dem doppelstöckigen Aussichtsboot der Lianshulu Lodge aus beobachten.*
A DROITE *Le ponton de Lianshulu Lodge permet d'observer en tout confort les nombreux oiseaux de l'East Caprivi.*

ABOVE *Curiosity draws the attention of the women and children of a small village in the Caprivi Strip.*

OBEN *Neugier fesselt die Aufmerksamkeit der Frauen und Kinder in einem kleinen Dorf im Caprivi-Streifen.*

CI-DESSUS *La curiosité l'emporte parmi les femmes et enfants de ce petit village dans la Caprivi Strip.*